This Notebook
Belongs To:

_____  -

_____

live MORE worry LESS

Time to head back to Amazon to order another book. If you enjoyed this notebook, we hope you will share your opinion by leaving a review on Amazon.
Thank you,
Inspired Lines

www.ingramcontent.com/pod-product-compliance
Lightning Source LLC
Chambersburg PA
CBHW070612220526
45467CB00003B/1393

* 9 7 8 1 7 0 4 8 0 8 6 0 4 *